BIG BOOK OF TRUCKS

by Patricia Relf
Illustrated by Thomas LaPadula

Cartwheel
·B·O·O·K·S· ®

SCHOLASTIC INC.
New York Toronto London Auckland Sydney

For Jack, Grace, Stephen, and Carrie
— P.R.

For Matthew and Alyse
— T.L.

Tonka® and Tonka® logo are trademarks of Hasbro, Inc. Copyright © 1996 Hasbro, Inc.
All rights reserved. Published by Scholastic Inc., 555 Broadway, New York, NY 10012.
CARTWHEEL BOOKS and the CARTWHEEL BOOKS logo
are registered trademarks of Scholastic Inc.

Library of Congress Cataloging-in-Publication Data

Relf, Patricia.
    Tonka big book of trucks / by Patricia Relf ; illustrated by Thomas LaPadula.
        p.   cm.
    "Cartwheel books" — T.p. verso.
    Summary: Text and illustrations describe all sorts of trucks used in building a house, on the highway, on a
farm, at a fire, and in other places.
    ISBN 0-590-84572-1
    1. Trucks — Juvenile literature. [1. Trucks.] I. LaPadula, Thomas, ill. II. Tonka Corporation. III. Title.
TL230.15.R45   1996
629.225 — dc20   95-47928
                                                                                                      CIP
                                                                                                       AC

12 11 10 9 8 7 6   9/9 0 1/0

Printed in Mexico   49

First Scholastic printing, September 1996

Contents

Building a House

Trucks work hard to build a new house. A backhoe digs a huge hole that will be the house's basement. A cement mixer brings concrete to make the floor and walls. A front loader carries a tree to its new spot. A bulldozer pushes the piles of dirt away, making a smooth yard for the house.

Building a House

LOADER

A loader works hard doing all kinds of jobs. Its shovel can scoop, dump, push, and carry heavy loads. Its big wheels roll right over rocks, lumps, and bumps. The operator sits inside the cab and uses a lever to move the bucket.

BACKHOE

A backhoe digs the earth with a sharp claw. Its arm bends in three places — like your shoulder, elbow, and wrist. It pulls its claw and bucket back and down, digging deep into the ground. Then it lifts its bucket and dumps the dirt in a pile nearby.

8

BULLDOZER

A bulldozer pushes dirt and rocks to make the ground smooth. Its sharp blade cuts through the hardest soil. Crawler tracks spread out the bulldozer's weight and let it push hard without getting stuck. The operator steers by using a lever to control each track.

CEMENT MIXER

A cement mixer, or ready-mix truck, carries fresh concrete to the building site. Its big drum turns, mixing the concrete as the truck drives to the building site. The driver adds water from a small tank to make the slushy mixture just right. Then the concrete flows out of the drum down a long chute.

Cement is a powder made by burning lime from limestone and silica from sand together with other ingredients. Cement mixed with sand, gravel, and water makes concrete. When it dries, concrete is almost as hard as stone. Many basements, sidewalks, roads, and even whole buildings are made of concrete.

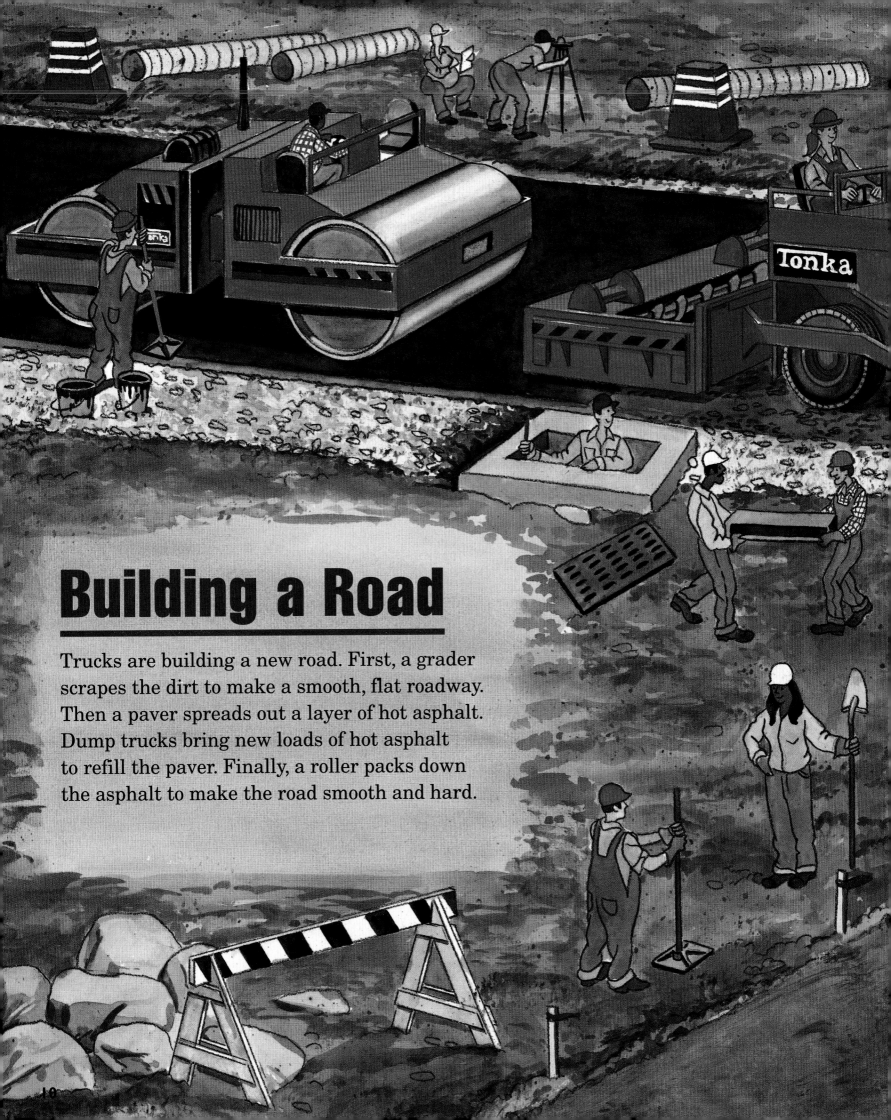

Building a Road

Trucks are building a new road. First, a grader scrapes the dirt to make a smooth, flat roadway. Then a paver spreads out a layer of hot asphalt. Dump trucks bring new loads of hot asphalt to refill the paver. Finally, a roller packs down the asphalt to make the road smooth and hard.

Building a Road

PAVER

A paver spreads a layer of hot asphalt on the ground just the way a knife spreads icing on a cake. A dump truck drops asphalt into the hopper at the front of the paver. Inside, a conveyor moves the asphalt to the back where a long bar called a screed spreads it evenly on the ground. After the asphalt cools, it will make a hard, strong surface for cars and trucks to drive on.

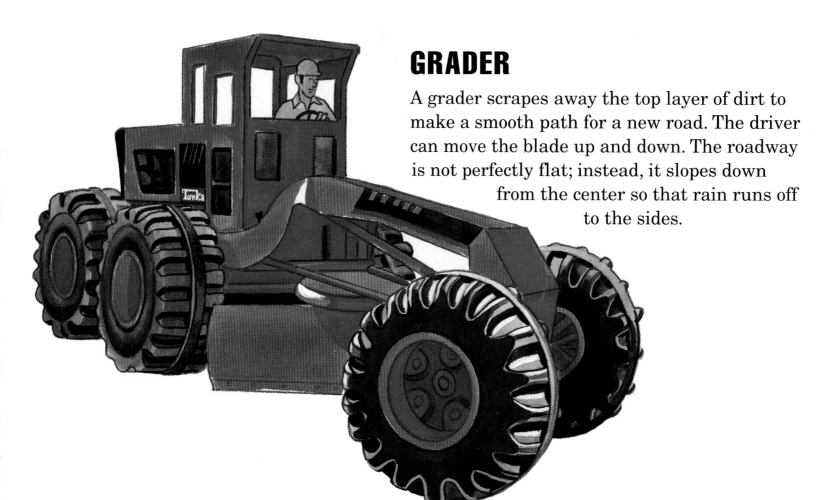

GRADER

A grader scrapes away the top layer of dirt to make a smooth path for a new road. The driver can move the blade up and down. The roadway is not perfectly flat; instead, it slopes down from the center so that rain runs off to the sides.

In the City

MOVING VAN

A moving van can hold everything from a house or apartment. Movers unload furniture and boxes full of dishes, clothes, toys, and books through doors at the back and side. Special pads cover each piece of furniture so that nothing will scratch it.

CHERRY PICKER

The cherry picker gets its name from the way it lifts a worker high in the air — high enough to pick cherries at the top of a tree. In the city, a cherry picker lifts a worker up to repair electrical wires or streetlights. The worker climbs into the bucket and uses the controls inside to move the bucket in any direction.

POLICE VAN

When many police officers are needed to control a crowd, the officers travel in police vans. A police van can also take anyone who is arrested back to the police station. The van has long benches and a partition to separate the driver from the people sitting in back.

STREET CLEANER

A street cleaner drives along the curb, sweeping up dirt and litter. Its big, turning brushes whisk the dirt into the truck's big tank. A spray of water helps to keep dust from flying into the air. Later, the truck will empty the dirt at a garbage dump.

Moving vans carry delicate things—boxes of dishes, fancy furniture, televisions, and computers. To make the ride more gentle and less bouncy, many moving vans have air bags, like big balloons, on the rear axle. An axle is the rod on which a pair of wheels spins. The air bags act as cushions, squishing a little each time the truck hits a bump so that the trailer itself rides smoothly.

On the Farm

A field of hay is ready to cut. Hay is grass that is good food for animals. First, a mower cuts the hay. Then a hayrake piles the hay into rows and leaves it in the field to dry. In another field, a tractor pulls a baler to gather dry hay into big blocks called bales. A hay truck takes them to the barn for storage.

On the Farm

TRACTOR

A tractor is a farmer's most useful machine. With its powerful engine, it can pull almost anything. It pulls a seed drill at planting time, a baler at harvest time, or a plow to break up the soil after the harvest is done. It can even pull a tree stump out of the ground.

HAY MOWER

A hay mower is like a huge lawn mower. Its cutting blades, called sickle bars, can be nine feet long! A combine mower cuts the hay, then crushes the stalks so that they will dry faster. Then the tractor pulls a hayrake through the field. The prongs of the rake leave the hay in neat, fluffy windrows to dry.

BALER

The next day, the tractor pulls a baler along the windrows of dry hay. Long forks gather in the hay. Inside, the machine packs the hay into a huge block, or bale, then ties it tightly with strong twine. Like magic, the neat bale of hay pops out the back.

HAY TRUCK

The hay truck follows behind the baler. A stacking machine picks up each bale of hay and stacks it neatly. When the truck is full, it takes the bales to the barn. Now the horses and cows will have hay to eat all winter long.

Farmers spend a lot of time on their tractors. Some tractors have air-conditioned cabs to keep the farmer cool, and fancy sound systems to play music. Many tractors have strong headlights so that the farmer can work late into the night.

At the Seaport

At a busy harbor, a ship has just arrived. It carries cars, television sets, and other things made far away. Trucks help to move all of this cargo out of the ship's hold. Some of the cargo goes to a warehouse for storage. Other things go directly onto tractor trailer trucks, which will deliver them quickly to stores across the country.

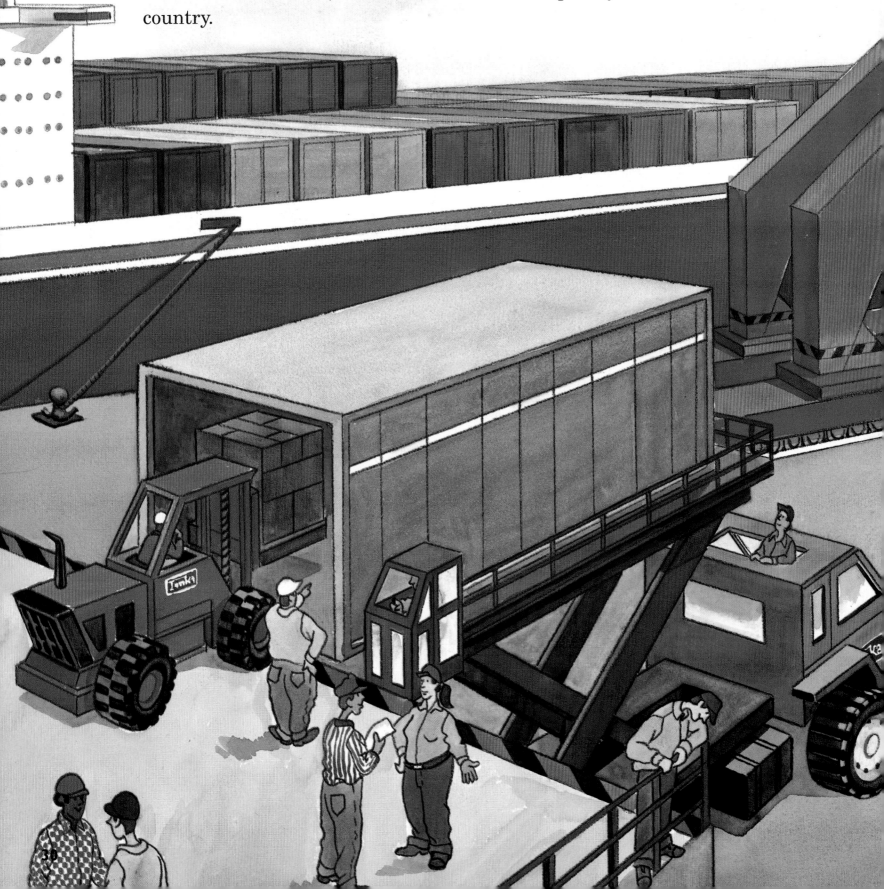

At the Seaport

FORKLIFT

A forklift carries boxes into a warehouse and stacks them. It has two prongs, like those on a fork, that scoop up crates from underneath. The small but powerful forklift can lift heavy loads higher than a person's head. Weights at the back prevent it from tipping over.

PLATFORM LOADER

A platform loader can lift a huge container, or many smaller boxes at once. It rolls a container into position, then raises it on a big, flat platform or floor. Its lifters open out like huge scissors blades.

GANTRY CRANE

The gantry crane unloads the biggest and heaviest crates. It lifts a crate out of the ship's hold, then moves the crate over the dock and lowers it. The gantry crane rolls along the dock on tracks, like a tall, slow train.

GRAPPLE TRUCK

A grapple truck has a claw that can pick up strangely shaped loads. It can carry anything from a bale of hay to a load of bricks or logs. The operator controls the arm and claw from a panel at the back of the truck.

Gantry means a span that stands over something, like a bridge. A gantry crane's legs are so tall and so far apart that other vehicles can drive under them, as if they were driving under a bridge!

At the State Fair

It's almost time for the state fair! The Ferris wheel arrives in pieces on a gooseneck trailer, ready to be assembled. A van pulls a food trailer to its spot on the midway. Outside the barns, owners unload their horses from a horse trailer. And monster trucks are already arriving for the first night's show.

At the State Fair

VENDING TRAILER

This vending trailer can serve ice cream to hundreds of fair visitors. A long freezer on one side of the trailer keeps ice cream and popsicles cold. Electrical power comes from a cable hooked up to an outside power supply. The trailer's own tank holds water for drinking and washing.

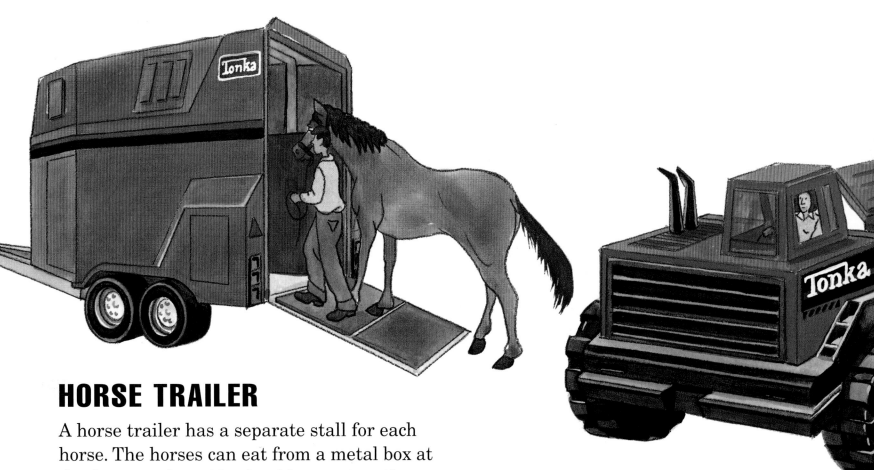

HORSE TRAILER

A horse trailer has a separate stall for each horse. The horses can eat from a metal box at the front as they ride. A rubber mat on the floor keeps the horses from sliding. The back door of the trailer opens out to make a ramp for the horses to walk up and down.

MONSTER TRUCK

A monster truck looks like an ordinary truck—until you see its huge wheels and tires! Those tires help it to climb over almost any obstacle and to plow through mud and dirt. A monster truck zooms up a dirt ramp, right over a line of old cars, and lands with a frightening bounce.

GOOSENECK TRAILER

A gooseneck trailer has an especially low deck to carry very heavy or very tall loads. It is often used to transport bulldozers and other heavy building machines. The front of the trailer stretches up to hook on to the tractor and looks a little like a goose's neck.

A county or state fair happens once a year, usually at the end of the summer. People from all over the state show off their animals, produce, and crafts. Everyone has fun at the shows and rides. The tallest Ferris wheel in the United States is at the Texas State Fair.

At a Fire

Fire trucks rush to a fire, sirens wailing. Firefighters climb ladders to rescue people from upper floors. Hoses attached to a pumper truck spray water to put out the fire. A rescue helicopter lifts people from the roof of the building. An ambulance is ready to help anyone who is hurt.

At a Fire

FIRE CHIEF'S TRUCK

The fire chief's truck is equipped with a radio to let the chief talk with firefighters inside a burning building, as well as with people back at headquarters. Like the other emergency vehicles, the chief's truck has flashing lights and a loud siren. These tell other drivers to pull to the side of the road and stop to let the fire trucks pass.

AMBULANCE

An ambulance carries everything needed to care for injured people and transport them to the hospital. A folding stretcher on wheels slides in through the back doors. Inside, there are medicines, bandages for wounds, and a tank of oxygen to help a patient breathe.

PUMPER

The pumper, or engine, is the first truck to leave the fire station on an emergency call. It carries the powerful water pump that can pump strong jets of water through several hoses at the same time. Hoses of different sizes are neatly folded at the back of the truck. The hoses are usually connected to a hydrant on the street, but the pumper carries its own tank of water, too.

LADDER TRUCK

The ladder truck carries a ladder that may reach five or six stories high. It can turn in any direction so that firefighters can reach every window. The truck also carries axes for breaking through doors and walls, poles with hooks for pulling down ceilings, and saws to cut holes in roofs and walls.

Most fire trucks are red, but in some cities emergency vehicles are painted bright yellow or yellowish-green. These colors are easy for other drivers to see. Fifty years ago, many fire trucks were painted blue!

At the Space Shuttle

The space shuttle is ready for another flight into space. A huge transporter slowly carries the shuttle more than three miles from the Vehicle Assembly Building to the launching pad. A van carries the workers who will fasten the shuttle, with its huge fuel tank and two rocket boosters, to the tall service structure.

At the Space Shuttle

CREW EGRESS TANK

A crew egress tank is ready to take the astronauts away from the launching pad in case there is an emergency before takeoff. The astronauts slide down a special slide, much like the emergency slide on a regular airplane, to escape from the shuttle.

VAN

A van moves ahead of the transporter to bring the engineers and other workers who will position the shuttle and check all of its working parts before takeoff. These checks take two or three days. This van may also bring astronauts to the shuttle on launch day!

FLATBED TRUCK

A giant flatbed truck with 40 wheels carries a satellite inside a special container. The satellite will be loaded into the shuttle's payload bay. Once the shuttle is in space, its payload bay doors will open and the satellite will be sent into space. For many years, the satellite will travel around the earth, sending telephone and television signals from one country to another.

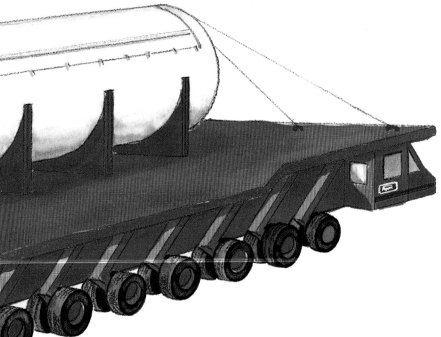

SHUTTLE TRANSPORTER

The shuttle transporter is the largest crawler truck in the world. It has eight crawler tracks, which move very slowly—about one mile an hour. You can walk much faster than that! Moving the shuttle to its launching pad may take more than five hours.

The space shuttle uses huge rockets to blast into space, but it drops the rockets once it is high enough. Then just the orbiter, the part that looks like an airplane, circles around the earth. When its mission is complete, the orbiter glides back into the earth's atmosphere and lands on a runway like an airplane.